Mamma

Tittie Go

Bye Bye

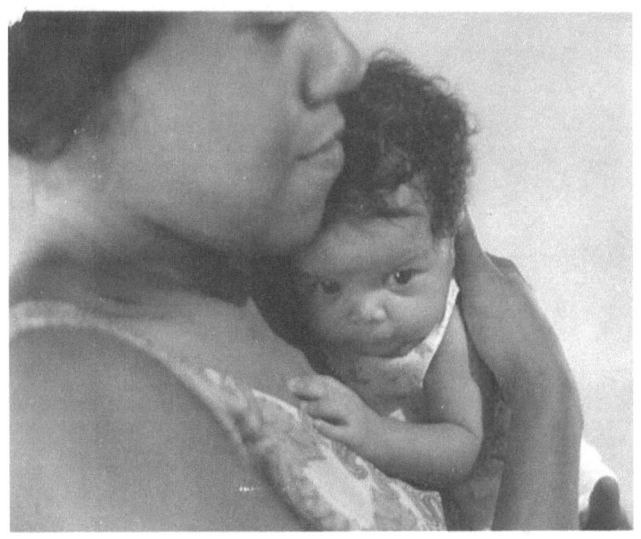

The pomes of Masibindi Mother Courage as compiled by Journaline Eastwind.

Copyright © 2021 by Journaline Eastwind
Published by Journaline Eastwind
Book Cover Design:
Eric Bell
Instagram: @ericcarleton
erixworld.com
PRINTED IN THE UNITED STATES OF AMERICA
ISBN 978-1-7373527-0-9

Dedication Page

Special thanks and love to Juana for keeping me sane.
Sunny for supporting me and being with me at my lowest ebb.
Eric for this bomb-ass cover.
Fritz my superlative editor.
Karaly who is 100%.
Heather and Meg, my sisters from other misters.
To all my friends who send late-night memes, funny videos and listen to me bitch.

                                                                I love you

Foreword

If you were blessed enough to know Masibindi Mother Courage, you were truly a very lucky person. Mother Masibindi never met a stranger, within the first few minutes you became a treasured friend, and she would do everything in her power to guide, soothe, love and befriend you. I had the privilege to know her over 6 years and it felt like I knew her all my life. That is the way she made you feel. I had just started my (retirement) job and they (her and her lovely daughter) were moving and needed some storage. We talked for over ten minutes and when I hung up I knew I had a lifelong loving friend. The next day they came in and reassured my initial feelings. Mother Masibindi was in my (and everyone she touched) opinion, a dear, caring, loving friend for life. She is missed and thought about every minute, of every hour of every day. She did so much for all who "were blessed enough to know her".

In conclusion, I would like to say," a Lady like this come around ONCE in a lifetime," In closing I would like to tell everyone who reads this that I feel like my life has been blessed by being able to say I had the privilege of being in her life

--Ed

Mama Tittie Go
Bye Bye

poems by:

Masibindi
Mother
Courage

8-22-05 - 8-22-12

Table of Contents

Dedication	iii
Foreword	iv
1. My Last week with 2 Breasts	1
2. 6/19/11 Father's Day	2
3. Ode to chemo	3
4. Happy Holidays	4
5. Mirror, Mirror	5
6. Attractiveness	6
7. Ode to Chemo	7
8. Mammaries, Mammaries	8
9. Mamma New Tittie Say "Hi Hi!"	9
10. Mama take some new medication	10
11. Happy Valentine's Day!	11
12. Oh Happy Day	13
13. Present For Ya	15
14. Why Mama Work When Mama Sick?	17
15. Chemo Cravin'	18
16. Burn, Witch, Burn	19
17. "Tumor" Fudd	20
18. 9-22-06	22
19. No Tittie No Pity	24
20. He's got a sick dick	26
21 Sufferin'	27
22 Skin 2 Skin	28
23 Uterus	29
24 Mama Eyes Weep	30
25 Cansa cansa everywhere	32
26 The Joys of Chemo	33
27 Where Mama Hair?	34
28 Mammaries Mammaries	35

29	Poem to Me	36
30	Mama anguish go bye bye	37
31	Holding Hands	38
32	Yo Mama so scary	39
33	Kwa heri	40
34	Consoling Words from Talking Turds aka Death Becomes You	41
35	Happy Holidays	42
36	Mama doctors can buy buy	44
37	Cancer =Cansa	45
38	Fall 2010	46
39	12-14-10	48
40	"Dinner Is Served"	49
41	SOS- I wan a DNA divorce	50
42	WWJD	51
	About The Author	53

My Last week with 2 Breasts
A Tale of 2 Titties

It was the last week I would have 2 breasts You could say that my life was really a mess
If only I'd had a man friend with comforting arms To rally me about my charms
To say "No matter what they cut off you, You're more woman with 1 than most with 2."

6/19/11 Father's Day

Thank you, LORD, for another day—
And for letting me live long enough for my hair to turn gray

A pome by Masibindi
6/19/11 Father's Day

Ode to chemo

Patches of hair gave me a scare Do I look like a baby?   Maybe. 53 years old—my head is cold. "No more nitro In my gravy!"

Happy Holidays

Christmas music is filling the air
It's hard not to whimper when your head has no hair
Where's the fun in food and tv sport
When your chest hurts from an infusaport? Listen
with glee to a carol's revision
Ignoring the pain from the breast mast' incision Gorge
new emeritus and fight a strong gag Enjoying the
humor of Santa's red stag
Merry Christmas to all and to all a good night Pray
for a reason not to give up the fight

Mirror, Mirror
with apologies to Snow White

Mirror Mirror on the wall Who's the
fairest of them all?
w/o left breast or mane of hair, chest
chemo port, & rank underwear Won't you
please forgive gall?
Can I be the fairest of them all? I tell
you now that you are fit Your physique's
taken quite a hit

Attractiveness

"You are so beautiful to me." Da
man sing on WKUT
Why do I feel so damn depressed Last time I
heard it I had both breasts hair on my body,
a song in my heart
Flimsy halters that made me look like a tart Talk
about a "skanky ho"
Prime "exhibit" for a freak show Head
as bald as my behind Jagged scar rivals
Frankenstein's Plastic port in my right
chest
Worthy of a "Creature Feature" guest Got
the runs (or else I cannot go) A prize
catch for any beau!
"Who cares how you look—what's important is your mind? To
your baldness & scar & port bulge I'm blind.
The chemo stench don't bother me at all I love
you, Dear—let's go to the mall."
"You've got inner beauty, a peaceful spirit..." All that
crap's a lot of bull shit
I look like a demon from the pit Without
hair or my left tit.

Ode to Chemo

Patches of hair gave me a scare Do I look like a baby?   Maybe. 53 years old...my head be cold – Not more nits in the gravy.

Mammaries, Mammaries

　　　just a hint of tit
Falsies; camisoles;
　　　　　　　　toilet paper roles;
Padding; pricy prosthetics;
　　　　　　　　a prayer to Jesus:
"Let my spirit soar in halter tops again."

Mamma New Tittie Say "Hi Hi!"

Mama new tittie say "Hi! Hi!" Mama
Kiss the blues "Bye Bye" Hold her bald
head up high, high Not sit around and
just sigh, sigh

Mama look up at the sky, sky
Say "Guess I'm not gonna die, die." "And if
I do, I won't cry, cry Spread my wings and
just fly, fly.

Mama take some new medication

Wow! Say goodbye to this constipation Avalide
– no more palpitation
Taxol reduced –cause for celebration.

Feel so good –just like tittie gone No
more self-pity –feelin' strong
See George Clinton, dance up and down Tell
bad jokes jes' like she's a clown.

Mama ready for sci fi convention Controllin'
stress and bad hypertension. Play a fun card
game called Magic— No mo' whinin' 'bout life
tragic.

Happy Valentine's Day!

Mama lookin' for new man. Tired of
usin' her right hand. Ready for a
wedding band.
So far, contenduhs been panned.

Most of options too young Some speak
with forked tongue Some would be
swell
Except for charnel house smell.

Some with IQ so low
Too kind to say that they "slow" Others
with teeth so rotten
Gums look like black manure-stained cotton

Breath contribute to global warming Sexual
predators, alarming Batterers are on the
prowl
Some men scare Mama with homely scowl Some
men lookin' for meal ticket
Others peepin' from a thicket Some
insane in the membrane
Druggies/alcoholics goin' down the drain

Don't go out and buy a dress for a weddin' It's
gonna be years befo' a beddin'
Mama tired of lookin' for new man Get some
mo' lotion for dat right hand

Oh Happy Day

This gaping socket on my chest Was once
a supple pliant breast. Now puckering skin
on jagged scar Resembles aftermath of
war.
A warm or spicy beverage
Sets nerve endings esophageal on edge My
armpit a half empty tomb
17 lymph nodes were removed. Halter
tops, I looked like a whore Now I am an
aging horror.
Without womb and my left breast— Tell
me Have I passed the test? Like Job I sit
alone and ponder
How much more pain 'til I git up yonder?

Present For Ya

I'm gonna piss on the world Now
that I'm a Lasex Girl

1-21-06   FTW

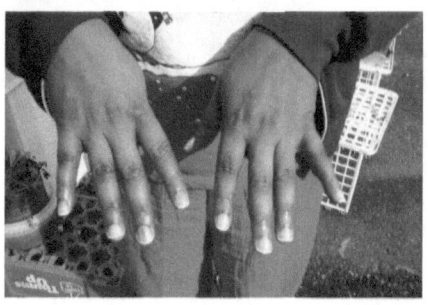

Umdlavuza cancer in Zulu

Why Mama Work When Mama Sick?

Mama teach at school each day
When she had hair, it was turnin' gray Now
umdlavuzi make her feel so bad But she ain't
got no Mom or Dad
Umdlavuzi turn her Mom & Nana insides into goo High
BP it bad + sissie had umdlavuzi, too
"Save us from extinction" Mama cry from the pew.

Why Mama work when Mama sick when we got SSI, Social
Security Disability and church aid from on high? Mama caint
get nuthin' & that's a sad fact
Though she's got a fatal illness, she not 'portant like Shaq.

They done give her Medicaid & wigs & scarves & food
"Fix yourself up ol' gal," they say, "That'll change your mood!"
You don't need help—you're fine!" they say, "Just exercise & work!" Tears
fill my eyes each time I see a heartless apathetic jerk.

So Mom gets up from bed of pain, insomnia and gas
She gags while washing hairless face & reflects on their nags She
pays the rent, electric, liability & dental amounting
Her past of abuse (bodily & mental's) discounted
"I gave you life," she says "you're mine to care for." So she
trudge to work to keep the wolf from the door.

Classroom management go bye bye Mom
look good in wig – she sigh Head make
her wanna cry, cry
Zap – caint look like herself esteem die, die
Students caint tell why, why

Chemo Cravin'

Give me Runts or give me death, Skittles,
Starbursts on my breath, Reese's Pieces,
candy corn;
Iced cake donuts
Clothing torn
Scale collapsing under weight Of my
seething chemo hate
                    Scathing
Vehement

1-23-06   Raa Middle School

Burn, Witch, Burn

7-7-06

They used to do it with fire Now
they use Tamoxifen

"Tumor" Fudd

Be very, very quiet: I'm
fightin' cancer

My eyes are always filled with tears Even
love don't calm my fears Tear-stained
hands in pain I raise
And do my best to give You praise.

9-22-06

Godby HS Here I
sit With 1 Tit
No longer feel like shit Cause I
retained my Wit

No Tittie No Pity

As I walk through the valley of the shadow of death I will
hold Your hand as I draw my last breath Then I will know
If I passed the Test
And I'll wait patiently for the rest.

9-24-06   St. Michael's Tallahassee

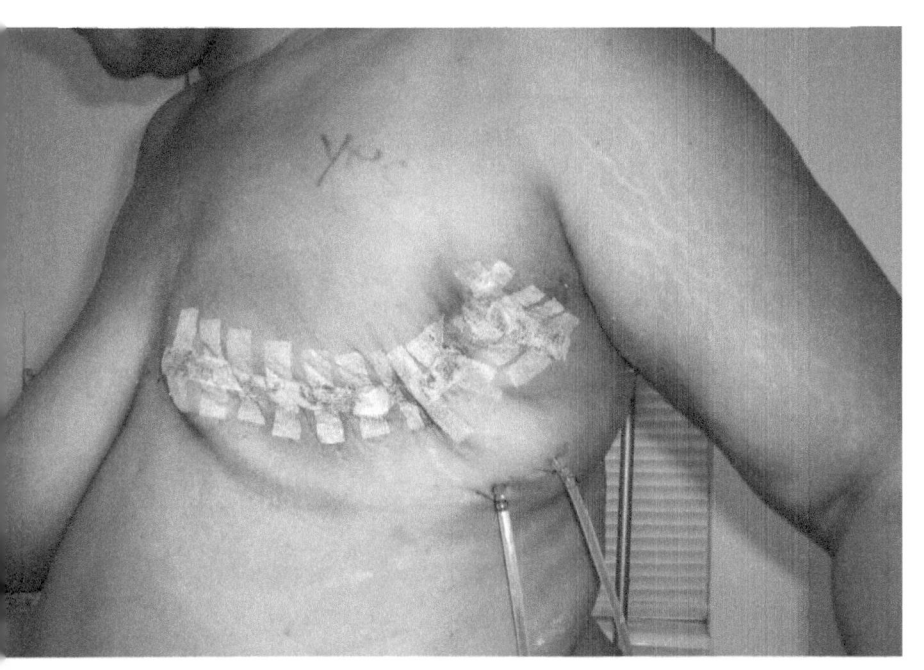

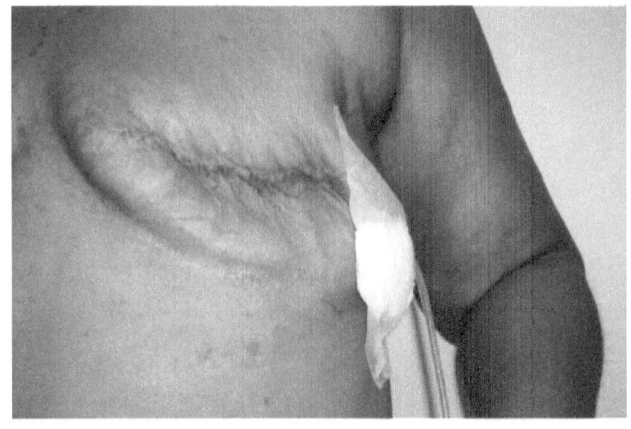

He's got a sick dick

And he is a sick prick So down
on my luck And I need a good
fuck

His cancer or mine? Amy
tit, his behind.
2 weddings - sex service has
cost me my cervix The uterus too
Cause they is dirty to screw

Set me free from the need It's been
years since I bleed Forgive me for
sin
Lust that burns so within Let me
finally have peace Play a game of
Sol Feace Leave the light on for
me Soon with You Lord I'll be

    7-16-06

Sufferin'

Saddens
Undermines
Frightens Frazzles
Embitters Robs
Interferes Negates

Skin 2 Skin

Mama you committed suicide by cancer you
smoke
you drank
you played the whore
Then said you Loved me more & more you
were a regular prancer
GrandMama you fought back with surgery & chemo you
smoke
you drank
you were a whore
yet you loved me more & more You were
a regular Captain Nemo

Uterus

Masi tittie go bye bye I boo
I hiss
I cry
You say I love earth less & less The mo'
they fill me with this mess An' I want to
die
I'm a regular American Pie

Mama Eyes Weep

Mama eyes weep for
                             womanity
On bus to work, and for
                             Manatee
Poison tears burn Mama
                             face

She weep 'bout Cansa in da
                             race
Womb – Man

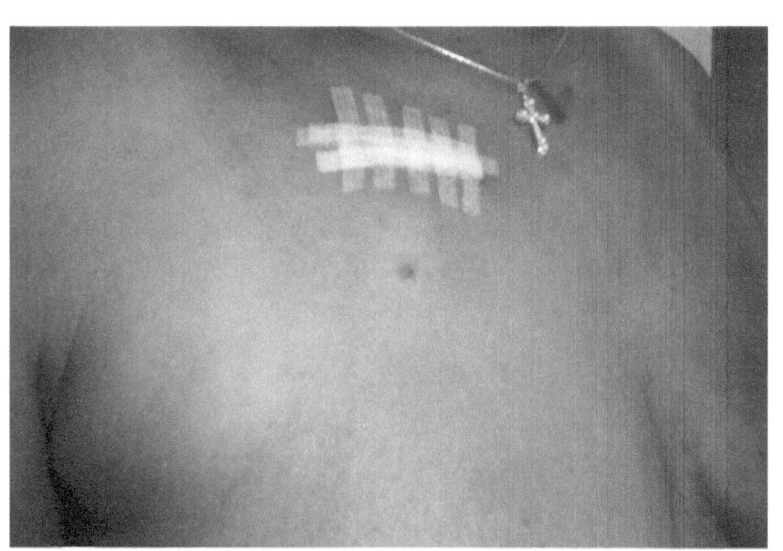

Cansa cansa everywhere

Cansa cansa people stare Tittie
gone
Hair gone, too
Plastic Port in right breast – whew Cansa
cansa everywhere
doctors rich beyond compare so I'll
say a little prayer!

The Joys of Chemo

White snot bleeds from blood-red eyes Sore &
Blackened inner thighs
Black half moons in finger nails
Spreading out like bloated snails

Where Mama Hair?

Mama find hair in dumpsta (fake) What look like it be combed by a rake Mama like da dumpsta hair
It soft enough for her to wear
2 rubber bands & hair 14 inches Mama look like story princess

Mammaries Mammaries
with apologies to "Memory" by Andrew Lloyd Webber

Justa Hint of Teat Falsies,
camisoles, Toilet Paper
Rolls,
Pricy Prosthesis, prayer to Jesus: Let my
spirit soar in halters again.

Poem to Me

I'm 55
Not filled with glee
I'm the chemo queen, u see labeled
by pathology
filled with ideology Yes I know
my A-b-c B.A.M.A., Ph.D.
tempered by theology
hindered by Biology
Left bra size now A – was D Chemo
port inside of me
hair on scalp – tee hee tee hee I'll
survive, oh yes, oui oui Trust in Jesus
is the Key

Mama anguish go bye bye

Cuz of her child, a small fry 36
hours to git her here
Fill Mama life with love and cheer

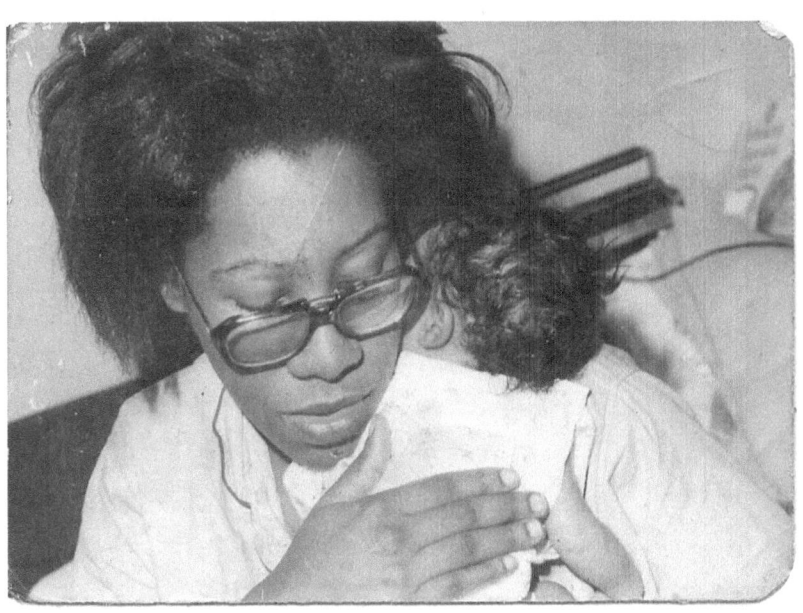

Holding Hands

God let 'em whack Mama tittie off
        To get her rapt attention She
was blissfully unaware
That she needed divine intervention.

She was maimed to make her whole Those
He loves He chastens
Now she's clinging to nail-scarred hands No
matter what she's facin'

Yo Mama so scary

Mama so scary sans hair & Tittie Me
afraid she will frighten Freddy

"Not as bad as Adriamycin with Cytoxin" Taxol
Smacks all

Kwa heri

It's time to go But God
says no
So I bear the Ankh-ology
A world that can't/won't pity me Like
some Kokomo Schmo

Consoling Words from Talking Turds aka Death Becomes You

"You look good!"
I may be dead in 3 months... "Yeah,
but you look good!"
I'll be a pretty corpse... "You
look so good!"
I don't give a fuck. I may be dying... "Yeah,
but you look good!"
It's not just the cancer that sucks— It's folk
so busy judging the outside
While cancer keeps on eatin' & creepin' 'til you die. I feel
like hell,
hate that cancer smell!
Get out of my face or say you'll pray I'll get well "Well, you look really good; you must be feelin' better!" Piss off!!!!!

Happy Holidays

Keep on rollin' with the flow "I will
not," I said "No!"
Gonna see Santa & put him to the test
All I want for Christmas is a healthy left breast And for
an encore 17 nodes
This port out of my chest & hair with 2 bows "Auld
sing syne" will make me wanna run
To the nearest pawn shop to buy me a gun

Then I saw Santa in his red suit & beard Old
tired eyes filled up with tears
It's ok, Dear, just gimme what you can give And I'll
do my best to try to want to live

Mama doctors can buy buy

All procedures are sky high
Mo 'ppointments than stars in the sky Mama
jes wan' to say bye bye

Mama $ go bye bye Tittie, hair
& she cry, cry
'hemo port in da one on the right Othuh
breast is out of sight

Mama act mean – make me cry cry Smell
like bad bar of soap, lye Scar on chest,
Frankenstein's bride Hair all gone, and huh
hurt pride

Mama lonely, she sigh, sigh Wan' a
man to be Kind, Kind Say he have to
be blind, blind Cause huh tittie go
bye, bye

Cancer =Cansa

Mama cansa say "hi hi" You or
I got to die die

Mama cansah go "hide!" "hide!" Lef' or
right caint dee-cide
Hemo – the – rapy wan' mah backside Mah
po cells get fried fried

Mama say she wan' ride ride God
say her plea denied
Sweet chariot past her done flied, flied God,
He aint never lied, lied

May say "sun not as bright, bright" Moon
don't light up the night, night Gettin'
cansa- and right, right Satan she wan' to
fight, fight

Fall 2010

Hold my Hand, Embrace
the Shell Save my Soul
from the fires of Hell

12-14-10
A pome by Messy Bindi

"A sensible question"
An open letter to the stuff inside That's
try to make me die:
May I ask you why?

"Dinner Is Served"
(with no apologies from your Orbital Mass)

You laugh; you lay; you pray; ebay;
par-tay at the cay; get up for day; bear a Blue Jay; write
letter K; go where you may; speak "yes & nay"
oncology by ray; spend your pay; think & say; go all the way! And
you try to kill me when all I do is eat?

SOS- I wan a DNA divorce

Tamoxifen Chemo Radiation – Nothing
works for your termination.

"More of you in my Life" Your
point is well taken– Flesh feasts
not forsaken.

WWJD

Yah Weh turned me from mourner to dancer: Why won't you help me get rid of this cancer?

Swell That I's well
Already done when I recreate you- Cancer flushed lower than gross number 2

Amen
OK - So be it

Waiting to die Care
for pie?
Got death on my eye. Could
it be a sty?
New cancer. Goodbye

12-1-10

Mom lost her battle August 22, 2012

About the Author:

Journaline Eastwind is Masibindi Mother Courage's daughter, caregiver and best friend. Mother Courage entrusted these poems to her as a part of her legacy.

www.ingramcontent.com/pod-product-compliance
Lightning Source LLC
Chambersburg PA
CBHW022110160426
43198CB00008B/423